MW01206196

ON SENSE AND THE SENSIBLE

by Aristotle

ON SENSE AND THE SENSIBLE

Table of Contents

ON SENSE AND THE SENSIBLE

by Aristotle

translated by J. I. Beare

Visit us at http://www.kessinger.net

1

HAVING now definitely considered the soul, by itself, and its several faculties, we must next make a survey of animals and all living things, in order to ascertain what functions are peculiar, and what functions are common, to them. What has been already determined respecting the soul [sc. by itself] must be assumed throughout. The remaining parts [sc. the attributes of soul and body conjointly] of our subject must be now dealt with, and we may begin with those that come first.

The most important attributes of animals, whether common to all or peculiar to some, are, manifestly, attributes of soul and body in conjunction, e.g. sensation, memory, passion, appetite and desire in general, and, in addition pleasure and pain. For these may, in fact, be said to belong to all animals. But there are, besides these, certain other attributes, of which some are common to all living things, while others are peculiar to certain species of animals. The most important of these may be summed up in four pairs, viz. waking and sleeping, youth and old age, inhalation and exhalation, life and death. We must endeavour to arrive at a scientific conception of these, determining their respective natures, and the causes of their occurrence.

But it behoves the Physical Philosopher to obtain also a clear view of the first principles of health and disease, inasmuch as neither health nor disease can exist in lifeless things. Indeed we may say of most physical inquirers, and of those physicians who study their art philosophically, that while the former complete their works with a disquisition on medicine, the latter usually base their medical theories on principles derived from Physics.

That all the attributes above enumerated belong to soul and body in conjunction, is obvious; for they all either imply sensation as a concomitant, or have it as their medium. Some are either affections or states of sensation, others, means of defending and safe–guarding it, while others, again, involve its destruction or negation. Now it is clear, alike by reasoning and observation, that sensation is generated in the soul through the medium of the body.

We have already, in our treatise On the Soul, explained the nature of sensation and the act of perceiving by sense, and the reason why this affection belongs to animals. Sensation must, indeed, be attributed to all animals as such, for by its presence or absence we distinguish essentially between what is and what is not an animal.

But coming now to the special senses severally, we may say that touch and taste necessarily appertain to all animals, touch, for the reason given in On the Soul, and taste, because of nutrition. It is by taste that one distinguishes in food the pleasant from the unpleasant, so as to flee from the latter and pursue the former: and savour in general is an affection of nutrient matter.

The senses which operate through external media, viz. smelling, hearing, seeing, are found in all animals which possess the faculty of locomotion. To all that possess them they are a means of preservation; their final cause being that such creatures may, guided by antecedent perception, both pursue their food, and shun things that are bad or destructive. But in animals which have also intelligence they serve for the attainment of a higher perfection. They bring in tidings of many distinctive qualities of things, from which the knowledge of truth, speculative and practical, is generated in the soul.

Of the two last mentioned, seeing, regarded as a supply for the primary wants of life, and in its direct effects, is the superior sense; but for developing intelligence, and in its indirect consequences, hearing takes the precedence. The faculty of seeing, thanks to the fact that all bodies are coloured, brings tidings of multitudes of distinctive qualities of all sorts; whence it is through this sense especially that we perceive the common sensibles, viz. figure, magnitude, motion, number: while hearing announces only the distinctive qualities of sound, and, to some few animals, those also of voice. indirectly, however, it is hearing that contributes most to the growth of intelligence. For rational discourse is a cause of instruction in virtue of its being audible, which it is, not directly, but indirectly; since it is composed of words, and each word is a thought–symbol. Accordingly, of persons destitute from birth of either sense, the blind are more intelligent than the deaf and dumb.

2

Of the distinctive potency of each of the faculties of sense enough has been said already.

But as to the nature of the sensory organs, or parts of the body in which each of the senses is naturally implanted, inquirers now usually take as their guide the fundamental elements of bodies. Not, however, finding it easy to coordinate five senses with four elements, they are at a loss respecting the fifth sense. But they hold the organ of sight to consist of fire, being prompted to this view by a certain sensory affection of whose true cause they are ignorant. This is that, when the eye is pressed or moved, fire appears to flash from it. This naturally takes place in darkness, or when the eyelids are closed, for then, too, darkness is produced.

This theory, however, solves one question only to raise another; for, unless on the hypothesis that a person who is in his full senses can see an object of vision without being aware of it, the eye must on this theory see itself. But then why does the above affection not occur also when the eye is at rest? The true explanation of this affection, which will contain the answer to our question, and account for the current notion that the eye consists of fire, must be determined in the following way: Things which are smooth have the natural property of shining in darkness, without, however, producing light. Now, the part of the eye called 'the black', i.e. its central part, is manifestly smooth. The phenomenon of the flash occurs only when the eye is moved, because only then could it possibly occur that the same one object should become as it were two. The rapidity of the movement has the effect of making that which sees and that which is seen seem different from one another. Hence the phenomenon does not occur unless the motion is rapid and takes place in darkness. For it is in the dark that that which is smooth, e.g. the heads of certain fishes, and the sepia of the cuttle–fish, naturally shines, and, when the movement of the eye is slow, it is impossible that that which sees and that which is seen should appear to be simultaneously two and one. But, in fact, the eye sees itself in the above phenomenon merely as it does so in ordinary optical reflexion.

If the visual organ proper really were fire, which is the doctrine of Empedocles, a doctrine taught also in the Timaeus, and if vision were the result of light issuing from the eye as from a lantern, why should the eye not have had the power of seeing even in the dark? It is totally idle to say, as the Timaeus does, that the visual ray coming forth in the darkness is quenched. What is the meaning of this 'quenching' of light? That which, like a fire of coals or an ordinary flame, is hot and dry is, indeed, quenched by the moist or cold; but heat and dryness are evidently not attributes of light. Or if they are attributes of it, but belong to it in a degree so slight as to be imperceptible to us, we should have expected that in the daytime the light of the sun should be quenched when rain falls, and that darkness should prevail in frosty weather. Flame, for example, and ignited bodies are subject to such extinction, but experience shows that nothing of this sort happens to the sunlight.

Empedocles at times seems to hold that vision is to be explained as above stated by light issuing forth from the eye, e.g. in the following passage:–

ON SENSE AND THE SENSIBLE

As when one who purposes going abroad prepares a lantern,
A gleam of fire blazing through the stormy night,
Adjusting thereto, to screen it from all sorts of winds,
    transparent sides,
Which scatter the breath of the winds as they blow,
While, out through them leaping, the fire,
    i.e. all the more subtile part of this,
Shines along his threshold old incessant beams:
So [Divine love] embedded the round "lens", [viz.]
    the primaeval fire fenced within the membranes,
In [its own] delicate tissues;
And these fended off the deep surrounding flood,
While leaping forth the fire, i.e. all its more subtile part–.

Sometimes he accounts for vision thus, but at other times he explains it by emanations from the visible objects.

Democritus, on the other hand, is right in his opinion that the eye is of water; not, however, when he goes on to explain seeing as mere mirroring. The mirroring that takes place in an eye is due to the fact that the eye is smooth, and it really has its seat not in the eye which is seen, but in that which sees. For the case is merely one of reflexion. But it would seem that even in his time there was no scientific knowledge of the general subject of the formation of images and the phenomena of reflexion. It is strange too, that it never occurred to him to ask why, if his theory be true, the eye alone sees, while none of the other things in which images are reflected do so.

True, then, the visual organ proper is composed of water, yet vision appertains to it not because it is so composed, but because it is translucent– a property common alike to water and to air. But water is more easily confined and more easily condensed than air; wherefore it is that the pupil, i.e. the eye proper, consists of water. That it does so is proved by facts of actual experience. The substance which flows from eyes when decomposing is seen to be water, and this in undeveloped embryos is remarkably cold and glistening. In sanguineous animals the white of the eye is fat and oily, in order that the moisture of the eye may be proof against freezing. Wherefore the eye is of all parts of the body the least sensitive to cold: no one ever feels cold in the part sheltered by the eyelids. The eyes of bloodless animals are covered with a hard scale which gives them similar protection.

It is, to state the matter generally, an irrational notion that the eye should see in virtue of something issuing from it; that the visual ray should extend itself all the way to the stars, or else go out merely to a certain point, and there coalesce, as some say, with rays which proceed from the object. It would be better to suppose this coalescence to take place in the fundament of the eye itself. But even this would be mere trifling. For what is meant by the 'coalescence' of light with light? Or how is it possible? Coalescence does not occur between any two things taken at random. And how could the light within the eye coalesce with that outside it? For the environing membrane comes between them.

That without light vision is impossible has been stated elsewhere; but, whether the medium between the eye and its objects is air or light, vision is caused by a process through this medium.

Accordingly, that the inner part of the eye consists of water is easily intelligible, water being translucent.

Now, as vision outwardly is impossible without [extra−organic] light, so also it is impossible inwardly [without light within the organ]. There must, therefore, be some translucent medium within the eye, and, as this is not air, it must be water. The soul or its perceptive part is not situated at the external surface of the eye, but obviously somewhere within: whence the necessity of the interior of the eye being translucent, i.e. capable of admitting light. And that it is so is plain from actual occurrences. It is matter of experience that soldiers wounded in battle by a sword slash on the temple, so inflicted as to sever the passages of [i.e. inward from] the eye, feel a sudden onset of darkness, as if a lamp had gone out; because what is called the pupil, i.e. the translucent, which is a sort of inner lamp, is then cut off [from its connexion with the soul].

Hence, if the facts be at all as here stated, it is clear that− if one should explain the nature of the sensory organs in this way, i.e. by correlating each of them with one of the four elements,− we must conceive that the part of the eye immediately concerned in vision consists of water, that the part immediately concerned in the perception of sound consists of air, and that the sense of smell consists of fire. (I say the sense of smell, not the organ.) For the organ of smell is only potentially that which the sense of smell, as realized, is actually; since the object of sense is what causes the actualization of each sense, so that it (the sense) must (at the instant of actualization) be (actually) that which before (the moment of actualization) it was potentially. Now, odour is a smoke−like evaporation, and smoke−like evaporation arises from fire. This also helps us to understand why the olfactory organ has its proper seat in the environment of the brain, for cold matter is potentially hot. In the same way must the genesis of the eye be explained. Its structure is an offshoot from the brain, because the latter is the moistest and coldest of all the bodily parts.

The organ of touch proper consists of earth, and the faculty of taste is a particular form of touch. This explains why the sensory organ of both touch and taste is closely related to the heart. For the heart as being the hottest of all the bodily parts, is the counterpoise of the brain.

This then is the way in which the characteristics of the bodily organs of sense must be determined.

3

Of the sensibles corresponding to each sensory organ, viz. colour, sound, odour, savour, touch, we have treated in On the Soul in general terms, having there determined what their function is, and what is implied in their becoming actualized in relation to their respective organs. We must next consider what account we are to give of any one of them; what, for example, we should say colour is, or sound, or odour, or savour; and so also respecting [the object of] touch. We begin with colour.

Now, each of them may be spoken of from two points of view, i.e. either as actual or as potential. We have in On the Soul explained in what sense the colour, or sound, regarded as actualized [for sensation] is the same as, and in what sense it is different from, the correlative sensation, the actual seeing or hearing. The point of our present discussion is, therefore, to determine what each sensible object must be in itself, in order to be perceived as it is in actual consciousness.

We have already in On the Soul stated of Light that it is the colour of the Translucent, [being so related to it] incidentally; for whenever a fiery element is in a translucent medium presence there is Light; while the privation of it is Darkness. But the 'Translucent', as we call it, is not something peculiar to air, or water, or any other of the bodies usually called translucent, but is a common 'nature' and power, capable of no separate existence of its own, but residing in these, and subsisting likewise in all other bodies in a greater or less degree. As the bodies in which it subsists must have some extreme bounding surface, so too must this. Here, then, we may say that Light is a 'nature' inhering in the Translucent when the latter is without determinate boundary. But it is manifest that, when the Translucent is in determinate bodies, its bounding extreme must be something real; and that colour is just this 'something' we are plainly taught by facts—colour being actually either at the external limit, or being itself that limit, in bodies. Hence it was that the Pythagoreans named the superficies of a body its 'hue', for 'hue', indeed, lies at the limit of the body; but the limit of the body; is not a real thing; rather we must suppose that the same natural substance which, externally, is the vehicle of colour exists [as such a possible vehicle] also in the interior of the body.

Air and water, too [i.e. as well as determinately bounded bodies] are seen to possess colour; for their brightness is of the nature of colour. But the colour which air or sea presents, since the body in which it resides is not determinately bounded, is not the same when one approaches and views it close by as it is when one regards it from a distance; whereas in determinate bodies the colour presented is definitely fixed, unless, indeed, when the atmospheric environment causes it to change. Hence it is clear that that in them which is susceptible of colour is in both cases the same. It is therefore the Translucent, according to the degree to which it subsists in bodies (and it does so in all more or less), that causes them to partake of colour. But since the colour is at the extremity of the body, it must be at the extremity of the Translucent in the body. Whence it follows that we may define colour as the limit of the Translucent in determinately bounded body. For whether we consider the special class of bodies called translucent, as water and such others, or determinate bodies, which appear to possess a fixed colour of their own, it is at the exterior bounding surface that all alike exhibit their colour.

Now, that which when present in air produces light may be present also in the Translucent which pervades determinate bodies; or again, it may not be present, but there may be a privation of it. Accordingly, as in the case of air the one condition is light, the other darkness, in the same way the colours White and Black are generated in determinate bodies.

We must now treat of the other colours, reviewing the several hypotheses invented to explain their genesis.

(1) It is conceivable that the White and the Black should be juxtaposed in quantities so minute that [a particle of] either separately would be invisible, though the joint product [of two particles, a black and a white] would be visible; and that they should thus have the other colours for resultants. Their product could, at all events, appear neither white nor black; and, as it must have some colour, and can have neither of these, this colour must be of a mixed character– in fact, a species of colour different from either. Such, then, is a possible way of conceiving the existence of a plurality of colours besides the White and Black; and we may suppose that [of this 'plurality'] many are the result of a [numerical] ratio; for the blacks and whites may be juxtaposed in the ratio of 3 to 2 or of 3 to 4, or in ratios expressible by other numbers; while some may be juxtaposed according to no numerically expressible ratio, but according to some relation of excess or defect in which the blacks and whites involved would be incommensurable quantities; and, accordingly, we may regard all these colours [viz. all those based on numerical ratios] as analogous to the sounds that enter into music, and suppose that those involving

simple numerical ratios, like the concords in music, may be those generally regarded as most agreeable; as, for example, purple, crimson, and some few such colours, their fewness being due to the same causes which render the concords few. The other compound colours may be those which are not based on numbers. Or it may be that, while all colours whatever [except black and white] are based on numbers, some are regular in this respect, others irregular; and that the latter [though now supposed to be all based on numbers], whenever they are not pure, owe this character to a corresponding impurity in [the arrangement of] their numerical ratios. This then is one conceivable hypothesis to explain the genesis of intermediate colours.

(2) Another is that the Black and White appear the one through the medium of the other, giving an effect like that sometimes produced by painters overlaying a less vivid upon a more vivid colour, as when they desire to represent an object appearing under water or enveloped in a haze, and like that produced by the sun, which in itself appears white, but takes a crimson hue when beheld through a fog or a cloud of smoke. On this hypothesis, too, a variety of colours may be conceived to arise in the same way as that already described; for between those at the surface and those underneath a definite ratio might sometimes exist; in other cases they might stand in no determinate ratio. To [introduce a theory of colour which would set all these hypotheses aside, and] say with the ancients that colours are emanations, and that the visibility of objects is due to such a cause, is absurd. For they must, in any case, explain sense–perception through Touch; so that it were better to say at once that visual perception is due to a process set up by the perceived object in the medium between this object and the sensory organ; due, that is, to contact [with the medium affected,] not to emanations.

If we accept the hypothesis of juxtaposition, we must assume not only invisible magnitude, but also imperceptible time, in order that the succession in the arrival of the stimulatory movements may be unperceived, and that the compound colour seen may appear to be one, owing to its successive parts seeming to present themselves at once. On the hypothesis of superposition, however, no such assumption is needful: the stimulatory process produced in the medium by the upper colour, when this is itself unaffected, will be different in kind from that produced by it when affected by the underlying colour. Hence it presents itself as a different colour, i.e. as one which is neither white nor black. So that, if it is impossible to suppose any magnitude to be invisible, and we must assume that there is some distance from which every magnitude is visible, this superposition theory, too [i.e. as well as No. 3 infra], might pass as a real theory of colour–mixture.

Indeed, in the previous case also there is no reason why, to persons at a distance from the juxtaposed blacks and whites, some one colour should not appear to present itself as a blend of both. [But it would not be so on a nearer view], for it will be shown, in a discussion to be undertaken later on, that there is no magnitude absolutely invisible.

(3) There is a mixture of bodies, however, not merely such as some suppose, i.e. by juxtaposition of their minimal parts, which, owing to [the weakness of our] sense, are imperceptible by us, but a mixture by which they [i.e. the 'matter' of which they consist] are wholly blent together by interpenetration, as we have described it in the treatise on Mixture, where we dealt with this subject generally in its most comprehensive aspect. For, on the supposition we are criticizing, the only totals capable of being mixed are those which are divisible into minimal parts, [e.g. genera into individuals] as men, horses, or the [various kinds of] seeds. For of mankind as a whole the individual man is such a least part; of horses [as an aggregate] the individual horse. Hence by the juxtaposition of these we obtain a mixed total, consisting [like a troop of cavalry] of both together; but we do not say that by such a process any individual man has been mixed with any individual horse. Not in this way, but by complete interpenetration [of their matter], must we conceive those things to be mixed which are not divisible into minima; and it is in the case of these that natural mixture exhibits itself in its most perfect form. We have explained already in our discourse 'On Mixture' how such mixture is possible. This being the true nature of mixture, it is plain that when bodies are mixed their colours also are necessarily mixed at the same time; and [it is no less plain] that this is the real cause determining the existence of a plurality of colours– not superposition or juxtaposition. For when bodies are thus mixed, their resultant colour presents itself as one and the same at all distances alike; not varying as it is seen nearer or farther away.

Colours will thus, too [as well as on the former hypotheses], be many in number on account of the fact that the ingredients may be combined with one another in a multitude of ratios; some will be based on determinate numerical ratios, while others again will have as their basis a relation of quantitative excess or defect not expressible in integers. And all else that was said in reference to the colours, considered as juxtaposed or superposed, may be said of them likewise when regarded as mixed in the way just described.

Why colours, as well as savours and sounds, consist of species determinate [in themselves] and not infinite [in number] is a question which we shall discuss hereafter.

4

We have now explained what colour is, and the reason why there are many colours; while before, in our work On the Soul, we explained the nature of sound and voice. We have next to speak of Odour and Savour, both of which are almost the same physical affection, although they each have their being in different things. Savours, as a class, display their nature more clearly to us than Odours, the cause of which is that the olfactory sense of man is inferior in acuteness to that of the lower animals, and is, when compared with our other senses, the least perfect of Man's sense of Touch, on the contrary, excels that of all other animals in fineness, and Taste is a modification of Touch.

Now the natural substance water per se tends to be tasteless. But [since without water tasting is impossible] either (a) we must suppose that water contains in itself [uniformly diffused through it] the various kinds of savour, already formed, though in amounts so small as to be imperceptible, which is the doctrine of Empedocles; or (b) the water must be a sort of matter, qualified, as it were, to produce germs of savours of all kinds, so that all kinds of savour are generated from the water, though different kinds from its different parts, or else (c) the water is in itself quite undifferentiated in respect of savour [whether developed or undeveloped], but some agent, such for example as one might conceive Heat or the Sun to be, is the efficient cause of savour.

(a) Of these three hypotheses, the falsity of that held by Empedocles is only too evident. For we see that when pericarpal fruits are plucked [from the tree] and exposed in the sun, or subjected to the action of fire, their sapid juices are changed by the heat, which shows that their qualities are not due to their drawing anything from the water in the ground, but to a change which they undergo within the pericarp itself; and we see, moreover, that these juices, when extracted and allowed to lie, instead of sweet become by lapse of time harsh or bitter, or acquire savours of any and every sort; and that, again, by the process of boiling or fermentation they are made to assume almost all kinds of new savours.

(b) It is likewise impossible that water should be a material qualified to generate all kinds of Savour germs [so that different savours should arise out of different parts of the water]; for we see different kinds of taste generated from the same water, having it as their nutriment.

(C) It remains, therefore, to suppose that the water is changed by passively receiving some affection from an external agent. Now, it is manifest that water does not contract the quality of sapidity from the agency of Heat alone. For water is of all liquids the thinnest, thinner even than oil itself, though oil, owing to its viscosity, is more ductile than water, the latter being uncohesive in its particles; whence water is more difficult than oil to hold in the hand without spilling. But since perfectly pure water does not, when subjected to the action of Heat, show any tendency to acquire consistency, we must infer that some other agency than heat is the cause of sapidity. For all savours [i.e. sapid liquors] exhibit a comparative consistency. Heat is, however, a coagent in the matter.

Now the sapid juices found in pericarpal fruits evidently exist also in the earth. Hence many of the old natural philosophers assert that water has qualities like those of the earth through which it flows, a fact especially manifest in the case of saline springs, for salt is a form of earth. Hence also when liquids are filtered through ashes, a bitter substance, the taste they yield is bitter. There are many wells, too, of which some are bitter, others acid, while others exhibit other tastes of all kinds.

As was to be anticipated, therefore, it is in the vegetable kingdom that tastes occur in richest variety. For, like all things else, the Moist, by nature's law, is affected only by its contrary; and this contrary is the Dry. Thus we see why the Moist is affected by Fire, which as a natural substance, is dry. Heat is, however, the essential property of Fire, as Dryness is of Earth, according to what has been said in our treatise on the elements. Fire and Earth, therefore, taken absolutely as such, have no natural power to affect, or be affected by, one another; nor have any other pair of substances. Any two things can affect, or be affected by, one another only so far as contrariety to the other resides in either of them.

As, therefore, persons washing Colours or Savours in a liquid cause the water in which they wash to acquire such a quality [as that of the colour or savour], so nature, too, by washing the Dry and Earthy in the Moist, and by filtering the latter, that is, moving it on by the agency of heat through the dry and earthy, imparts to it a certain quality. This affection, wrought by the aforesaid Dry in the Moist, capable of transforming the sense of Taste from potentiality to actuality, is Savour. Savour brings into actual exercise the perceptive faculty which pre–existed only in potency. The activity of sense–perception in general is analogous, not to the process of acquiring knowledge, but to that of exercising knowledge already acquired.

ON SENSE AND THE SENSIBLE

That Savours, either as a quality or as the privation of a quality, belong not to every form of the Dry but to the Nutrient, we shall see by considering that neither the Dry without the Moist, nor the Moist without the Dry, is nutrient. For no single element, but only composite substance, constitutes nutriment for animals. Now, among the perceptible elements of the food which animals assimilate, the tangible are the efficient causes of growth and decay; it is qua hot or cold that the food assimilated causes these; for the heat or cold is the direct cause of growth or decay. It is qua gustable, however, that the assimilated food supplies nutrition. For all organisms are nourished by the Sweet [i.e. the 'gustable' proper], either by itself or in combination with other savours. Of this we must speak with more precise detail in our work on Generation: for the present we need touch upon it only so far as our subject here requires. Heat causes growth, and fits the food–stuff for alimentation; it attracts [into the organic system] that which is light [viz. the sweet], while the salt and bitter it rejects because of their heaviness. In fact, whatever effects external heat produces in external bodies, the same are produced by their internal heat in animal and vegetable organisms. Hence it is [i.e. by the agency of heat as described] that nourishment is effected by the sweet. The other savours are introduced into and blended in food [naturally] on a principle analogous to that on which the saline or the acid is used artificially, i.e. for seasoning. These latter are used because they counteract the tendency of the sweet to be too nutrient, and to float on the stomach.

As the intermediate colours arise from the mixture of white and black, so the intermediate savours arise from the Sweet and Bitter; and these savours, too, severally involve either a definite ratio, or else an indefinite relation of degree, between their components, either having certain integral numbers at the basis of their mixture, and, consequently, of their stimulative effect, or else being mixed in proportions not arithmetically expressible. The tastes which give pleasure in their combination are those which have their components joined in a definite ratio.

The sweet taste alone is Rich, [therefore the latter may be regarded as a variety of the former], while [so far as both imply privation of the Sweet] the Saline is fairly identical with the Bitter. Between the extremes of sweet and bitter come the Harsh, the Pungent, the Astringent, and the Acid. Savours and Colours, it will be observed, contain respectively about the same number of species. For there are seven species of each, if, as is reasonable, we regard Dun [or Grey] as a variety of Black (for the alternative is that Yellow should be classed with White, as Rich with Sweet); while [the irreducible colours, viz.] Crimson, Violet, leek–Green, and deep Blue, come between White and

14

Black, and from these all others are derived by mixture.

Again, as Black is a privation of White in the Translucent, so Saline or Bitter is a privation of Sweet in the Nutrient Moist. This explains why the ash of all burnt things is bitter; for the potable [sc. the sweet] moisture has been exuded from them.

Democritus and most of the natural philosophers who treat of sense–perception proceed quite irrationally, for they represent all objects of sense as objects of Touch. Yet, if this is really so, it clearly follows that each of the other senses is a mode of Touch; but one can see at a glance that this is impossible.

Again, they treat the percepts common to all senses as proper to one. For [the qualities by which they explain taste viz.] Magnitude and Figure, Roughness and Smoothness, and, moreover, the Sharpness and Bluntness found in solid bodies, are percepts common to all the senses, or if not to all, at least to Sight and Touch. This explains why it is that the senses are liable to err regarding them, while no such error arises respecting their proper sensibles; e.g. the sense of Seeing is not deceived as to Colour, nor is that of Hearing as to Sound.

On the other hand, they reduce the proper to common sensibles, as Democritus does with White and Black; for he asserts that the latter is [a mode of the] rough, and the former [a mode of the] smooth, while he reduces Savours to the atomic figures. Yet surely no one sense, or, if any, the sense of Sight rather than any other, can discern the common sensibles. But if we suppose that the sense of Taste is better able to do so, then– since to discern the smallest objects in each kind is what marks the acutest sense–Taste should have been the sense which best perceived the common sensibles generally, and showed the most perfect power of discerning figures in general.

Again, all the sensibles involve contrariety; e.g. in Colour White is contrary to Black, and in Savours Bitter is contrary to Sweet; but no one figure is reckoned as contrary to any other figure. Else, to which of the possible polygonal figures [to which Democritus reduces Bitter] is the spherical figure [to which he reduces Sweet] contrary?

Again, since figures are infinite in number, savours also should be infinite; [the possible rejoinder– 'that they are so, only that some are not perceived'– cannot be sustained] for why should one savour be perceived, and another not?

This completes our discussion of the object of Taste, i.e. Savour; for the other affections of Savours are examined in their proper place in connection with the natural history of Plants.

5

Our conception of the nature of Odours must be analogous to that of Savours; inasmuch as the Sapid Dry effects in air and water alike, but in a different province of sense, precisely what the Dry effects in the Moist of water only. We customarily predicate Translucency of both air and water in common; but it is not qua translucent that either is a vehicle of odour, but qua possessed of a power of washing or rinsing [and so imbibing] the Sapid Dryness.

For the object of Smell exists not in air only: it also exists in water. This is proved by the case of fishes and testacea, which are seen to possess the faculty of smell, although water contains no air (for whenever air is generated within water it rises to the surface), and these creatures do not respire. Hence, if one were to assume that air and water are both moist, it would follow that Odour is the natural substance consisting of the Sapid Dry diffused in the Moist, and whatever is of this kind would be an object of Smell.

That the property of odorousness is based upon the Sapid may be seen by comparing the things which possess with those which do not possess odour. The elements, viz. Fire, Air, Earth, Water, are inodorous, because both the dry and the moist among them are without sapidity, unless some added ingredient produces it. This explains why sea−water possesses odour, for [unlike 'elemental' water] it contains savour and dryness. Salt, too, is more odorous than natron, as the oil which exudes from the former proves, for natron is allied to ['elemental'] earth more nearly than salt. Again, a stone is inodorous, just because it is tasteless, while, on the contrary, wood is odorous, because it is sapid. The kinds of wood, too, which contain more ['elemental'] water are less odorous than others. Moreover, to take the case of metals, gold is inodorous because it is without taste, but bronze and iron are odorous; and when the [sapid] moisture has been burnt out of them, their slag is, in all cases, less odorous the metals [than the metals themselves]. Silver and tin are more odorous than the one class of metals, less so than the other, inasmuch as they are water [to a greater degree than the former, to a less degree than the latter].

ON SENSE AND THE SENSIBLE

Some writers look upon Fumid exhalation, which is a compound of Earth and Air, as the essence of Odour. [Indeed all are inclined to rush to this theory of Odour.] Heraclitus implied his adherence to it when he declared that if all existing things were turned into Smoke, the nose would be the organ to discern them with. All writers incline to refer odour to this cause [sc. exhalation of some sort], but some regard it as aqueous, others as fumid, exhalation; while others, again, hold it to be either. Aqueous exhalation is merely a form of moisture, but fumid exhalation is, as already remarked, composed of Air and Earth. The former when condensed turns into water; the latter, in a particular species of earth. Now, it is unlikely that odour is either of these. For vaporous exhalation consists of mere water [which, being tasteless, is inodorous]; and fumid exhalation cannot occur in water at all, though, as has been before stated, aquatic creatures also have the sense of smell.

Again, the exhalation theory of odour is analogous to the theory of emanations. If, therefore, the latter is untenable, so, too, is the former.

It is clearly conceivable that the Moist, whether in air (for air, too, is essentially moist) or in water, should imbibe the influence of, and have effects wrought in it by, the Sapid Dryness. Moreover, if the Dry produces in moist media, i.e. water and air, an effect as of something washed out in them, it is manifest that odours must be something analogous to savours. Nay, indeed, this analogy is, in some instances, a fact [registered in language]; for odours as well as savours are spoken of as pungent, sweet, harsh, astringent rich [='savoury']; and one might regard fetid smells as analogous to bitter tastes; which explains why the former are offensive to inhalation as the latter are to deglutition. It is clear, therefore, that Odour is in both water and air what Savour is in water alone. This explains why coldness and freezing render Savours dull, and abolish odours altogether; for cooling and freezing tend to annul the kinetic heat which helps to fabricate sapidity.

There are two species of the Odorous. For the statement of certain writers that the odorous is not divisible into species is false; it is so divisible. We must here define the sense in which these species are to be admitted or denied.

One class of odours, then, is that which runs parallel, as has been observed, to savours: to odours of this class their pleasantness or unpleasantness belongs incidentally. For owing to the fact that Savours are qualities of nutrient matter, the odours connected with these [e.g. those of a certain food] are agreeable as long as animals have an appetite for the

17

food, but they are not agreeable to them when sated and no longer in want of it; nor are they agreeable, either, to those animals that do not like the food itself which yields the odours. Hence, as we observed, these odours are pleasant or unpleasant incidentally, and the same reasoning explains why it is that they are perceptible to all animals in common.

The other class of odours consists of those agreeable in their essential nature, e.g. those of flowers. For these do not in any degree stimulate animals to food, nor do they contribute in any way to appetite; their effect upon it, if any, is rather the opposite. For the verse of Strattis ridiculing Euripides—

ON SENSE AND THE SENSIBLE

Use not perfumery to flavour soup,

contains a truth.

Those who nowadays introduce such flavours into beverages deforce our sense of pleasure by habituating us to them, until, from two distinct kinds of sensations combined, pleasure arises as it might from one simple kind.

Of this species of odour man alone is sensible; the other, viz. that correlated with Tastes, is, as has been said before, perceptible also to the lower animals. And odours of the latter sort, since their pleasureableness depends upon taste, are divided into as many species as there are different tastes; but we cannot go on to say this of the former kind of odour, since its nature is agreeable or disagreeable per se. The reason why the perception of such odours is peculiar to man is found in the characteristic state of man's brain. For his brain is naturally cold, and the blood which it contains in its vessels is thin and pure but easily cooled (whence it happens that the exhalation arising from food, being cooled by the coldness of this region, produces unhealthy rheums); therefore it is that odours of such a species have been generated for human beings, as a safeguard to health. This is their sole function, and that they perform it is evident. For food, whether dry or moist, though sweet to taste, is often unwholesome; whereas the odour arising from what is fragrant, that odour which is pleasant in its own right, is, so to say, always beneficial to persons in any state of bodily health whatever.

For this reason, too, the perception of odour [in general] effected through respiration, not in all animals, but in man and certain other sanguineous animals, e.g. quadrupeds, and all that participate freely in the natural substance air; because when odours, on account of the lightness of the heat in them, mount to the brain, the health of this region is thereby promoted. For odour, as a power, is naturally heat–giving. Thus Nature has employed respiration for two purposes: primarily for the relief thereby brought to the thorax, secondarily for the inhalation of odour. For while an animal is inhaling,– odour moves in through its nostrils, as it were 'from a side–entrance.'

But the perception of the second class of odours above described [does not belong to all animal, but] is confined to human beings, because man's brain is, in proportion to his whole bulk, larger and moister than the brain of any other animal. This is the reason of the further fact that man alone, so to speak, among animals perceives and takes pleasure in the odours of flowers and such things. For the heat and stimulation set up by these odours are commensurate with the excess of moisture and coldness in his cerebral region.

ON SENSE AND THE SENSIBLE

On all the other animals which have lungs, Nature has bestowed their due perception of one of the two kinds of odour [i.e. that connected with nutrition] through the act of respiration, guarding against the needless creation of two organs of sense; for in the fact that they respire the other animals have already sufficient provision for their perception of the one species of odour only, as human beings have for their perception of both.

But that creatures which do not respire have the olfactory sense is evident. For fishes, and all insects as a class, have, thanks to the species of odour correlated with nutrition, a keen olfactory sense of their proper food from a distance, even when they are very far away from it; such is the case with bees, and also with the class of small ants, which some denominate knipes. Among marine animals, too, the murex and many other similar animals have an acute perception of their food by its odour.

It is not equally certain what the organ is whereby they so perceive. This question, of the organ whereby they perceive odour, may well cause a difficulty, if we assume that smelling takes place in animals only while respiring (for that this is the fact is manifest in all the animals which do respire), whereas none of those just mentioned respires, and yet they have the sense of smell– unless, indeed, they have some other sense not included in the ordinary five. This supposition is, however, impossible. For any sense which perceives odour is a sense of smell, and this they do perceive, though probably not in the same way as creatures which respire, but when the latter are respiring the current of breath removes something that is laid like a lid upon the organ proper (which explains why they do not perceive odours when not respiring); while in creatures which do not respire this is always off: just as some animals have eyelids on their eyes, and when these are not raised they cannot see, whereas hard–eyed animals have no lids, and consequently do not need, besides eyes, an agency to raise the lids, but see straightway [without intermission] from the actual moment at which it is first possible for them to do so [i.e. from the moment when an object first comes within their field of vision].

Consistently with what has been said above, not one of the lower animals shows repugnance to the odour of things which are essentially ill–smelling, unless one of the latter is positively pernicious. They are destroyed, however, by these things, just as human beings are; i.e. as human beings get headaches from, and are often asphyxiated by, the fumes of charcoal, so the lower animals perish from the strong fumes of brimstone and bituminous substances; and it is owing to experience of such effects that they shun these. For the disagreeable odour in itself they care nothing whatever (though the odours of many plants are essentially disagreeable), unless, indeed, it has some effect upon the taste of their food.

The senses making up an odd number, and an odd number having always a middle unit, the sense of smell occupies in itself as it were a middle position between the tactual senses, i.e. Touch and Taste, and those which perceive through a medium, i.e. Sight and Hearing. Hence the object of smell, too, is an affection of nutrient substances (which fall within the class of Tangibles), and is also an affection of the audible and the visible; whence it is that creatures have the sense of smell both in air and water. Accordingly, the object of smell is something common to both of these provinces, i.e. it appertains both to the tangible on the one hand, and on the other to the audible and translucent. Hence the propriety of the figure by which it has been described by us as an immersion or washing of dryness in the Moist and Fluid. Such then must be our account of the sense in which one is or is not entitled to speak of the odorous as having species.

The theory held by certain of the Pythagoreans, that some animals are nourished by odours alone, is unsound. For, in the first place, we see that food must be composite, since the bodies nourished by it are not simple. This explains why waste matter is secreted from food, either within the organisms, or, as in plants, outside them. But since even water by itself alone, that is, when unmixed, will not suffice for food— for anything which is to form a consistency must be corporeal—, it is still much less conceivable that air should be so corporealized [and thus fitted to be food]. But, besides this, we see that all animals have a receptacle for food, from which, when it has entered, the body absorbs it. Now, the organ which perceives odour is in the head, and odour enters with the inhalation of the breath; so that it goes to the respiratory region. It is plain, therefore, that odour, qua odour, does not contribute to nutrition; that, however, it is serviceable to health is equally plain, as well by immediate perception as from the arguments above employed; so that odour is in relation to general health what savour is in the province of nutrition and in relation to the bodies nourished.

This then must conclude our discussion of the several organs of sense—perception.

6

One might ask: if every body is infinitely divisible, are its sensible qualities— Colour,

ON SENSE AND THE SENSIBLE

Savour, Odour, Sound, Weight, Cold or Heat, [Heaviness or] Lightness, Hardness or Softness—also infinitely divisible? Or, is this impossible?

[One might well ask this question], because each of them is productive of sense–perception, since, in fact, all derive their name [of 'sensible qualities'] from the very circumstance of their being able to stimulate this. Hence, [if this is so] both our perception of them should likewise be divisible to infinity, and every part of a body [however small] should be a perceptible magnitude. For it is impossible, e.g. to see a thing which is white but not of a certain magnitude.

Since if it were not so, [if its sensible qualities were not divisible, pari passu with body], we might conceive a body existing but having no colour, or weight, or any such quality; accordingly not perceptible at all. For these qualities are the objects of sense–perception. On this supposition, every perceptible object should be regarded as composed not of perceptible [but of imperceptible] parts. Yet it must [be really composed of perceptible parts], since assuredly it does not consist of mathematical [and therefore purely abstract and non–sensible] quantities. Again, by what faculty should we discern and cognize these [hypothetical real things without sensible qualities]? Is it by Reason? But they are not objects of Reason; nor does reason apprehend objects in space, except when it acts in conjunction with sense–perception. At the same time, if this be the case [that there are magnitudes, physically real, but without sensible quality], it seems to tell in favour of the atomistic hypothesis; for thus, indeed, [by accepting this hypothesis], the question [with which this chapter begins] might be solved [negatively]. But it is impossible [to accept this hypothesis]. Our views on the subject of atoms are to be found in our treatise on Movement.

The solution of these questions will bring with it also the answer to the question why the species of Colour, Taste, Sound, and other sensible qualities are limited. For in all classes of things lying between extremes the intermediates must be limited. But contraries are extremes, and every object of sense–perception involves contrariety: e.g. in Colour, White x Black; in Savour, Sweet x Bitter, and in all the other sensibles also the contraries are extremes. Now, that which is continuous is divisible into an infinite number of unequal parts, but into a finite number of equal parts, while that which is not per se continuous is divisible into species which are finite in number. Since then, the several sensible qualities of things are to be reckoned as species, while continuity always subsists in these, we must take account of the difference between the Potential and the Actual. It

23

is owing to this difference that we do not [actually] see its ten—thousandth part in a grain of millet, although sight has embraced the whole grain within its scope; and it is owing to this, too, that the sound contained in a quarter—tone escapes notice, and yet one hears the whole strain, inasmuch as it is a continuum; but the interval between the extreme sounds [that bound the quarter—tone] escapes the ear [being only potentially audible, not actually]. So, in the case of other objects of sense, extremely small constituents are unnoticed; because they are only potentially not actually [perceptible e.g.] visible, unless when they have been parted from the wholes. So the footlength too exists potentially in the two—foot length, but actually only when it has been separated from the whole. But objective increments so small as those above might well, if separated from their totals, [instead of achieving 'actual' exisistence] be dissolved in their environments, like a drop of sapid moisture poured out into the sea. But even if this were not so [sc. with the objective magnitude], still, since the [subjective] of sense—perception is not perceptible in itself, nor capable of separate existence (since it exists only potentially in the more distinctly perceivable whole of sense—perception), so neither will it be possible to perceive [actually] its correlatively small object [sc. its quantum of pathema or sensible quality] when separated from the object—total. But yet this [small object] is to be considered as perceptible: for it is both potentially so already [i.e. even when alone], and destined to be actually so when it has become part of an aggregate. Thus, therefore, we have shown that some magnitudes and their sensible qualities escape notice, and the reason why they do so, as well as the manner in which they are still perceptible or not perceptible in such cases. Accordingly then when these [minutely subdivided] sensibles have once again become aggregated in a whole in such a manner, relatively to one another, as to be perceptible actually, and not merely because they are in the whole, but even apart from it, it follows necessarily [from what has been already stated] that their sensible qualities, whether colours or tastes or sounds, are limited in number.

One might ask:— do the objects of sense—perception, or the movements proceeding from them ([since movements there are,] in whichever of the two ways [viz. by emanations or by stimulatory kinesis] sense—perception takes place), when these are actualized for perception, always arrive first at a spatial middle point [between the sense—organ and its object], as Odour evidently does, and also Sound? For he who is nearer [to the odorous object] perceives the Odour sooner [than who is farther away], and the Sound of a stroke reaches us some time after it has been struck. Is it thus also with an object seen, and with Light? Empedocles, for example, says that the Light from the Sun arrives first in the intervening space before it comes to the eye, or reaches the Earth. This might plausibly seem to be the case. For whatever is moved [in space], is moved from one place to another; hence there must be a corresponding interval of time also in which it is moved from the one place to the other. But any given time is divisible into parts; so that we should assume a time when the sun's ray was not as yet seen, but was still travelling in the middle space.

Now, even if it be true that the acts of 'hearing' and 'having heard', and, generally, those of 'perceiving' and 'having perceived', form co−instantaneous wholes, in other words, that acts of sense−perception do not involve a process of becoming, but have their being none the less without involving such a process; yet, just as, [in the case of sound], though the stroke which causes the Sound has been already struck, the Sound is not yet at the ear (and that this last is a fact is further proved by the transformation which the letters [viz. the consonants as heard] undergo [in the case of words spoken from a distance], implying that the local movement [involved in Sound] takes place in the space between [us and the speaker]; for the reason why [persons addressed from a distance] do not succeed in catching the sense of what is said is evidently that the air [sound wave] in moving towards them has its form changed) [granting this, then, the question arises]: is the same also true in the case of Colour and Light? For certainly it is not true that the beholder sees, and the object is seen, in virtue of some merely abstract relationship between them, such as that between equals. For if it were so, there would be no need [as there is] that either [the beholder or the thing beheld] should occupy some particular place; since to the equalization of things their being near to, or far from, one another makes no difference.

Now this [travelling through successive positions in the medium] may with good reason take place as regards Sound and Odour, for these, like [their media] Air and Water, are continuous, but the movement of both is divided into parts. This too is the ground of the fact that the object which the person first in order of proximity hears or smells is the same as that which each subsequent person perceives, while yet it is not the same.

Some, indeed, raise a question also on these very points; they declare it impossible that one person should hear, or see, or smell, the same object as another, urging the impossibility of several persons in different places hearing or smelling [the same object], for the one same thing would [thus] be divided from itself. The answer is that, in perceiving the object which first set up the motion− e.g. a bell, or frankincense, or fire− all perceive an object numerically one and the same; while, of course, in the special object perceived they perceive an object numerically different for each, though specifically the same for all; and this, accordingly, explains how it is that many persons together see, or smell, or hear [the same object]. These things [the odour or sound proper] are not bodies, but an affection or process of some kind (otherwise this [viz. simultaneous perception of the one object by many] would not have been, as it is, a fact of experience) though, on the other hand, they each imply a body [as their cause].

But [though sound and odour may travel,] with regard to Light the case is different. For Light has its raison d'etre in the being [not becoming] of something, but it is not a movement. And in general, even in qualitative change the case is different from what it is in local movement [both being different species of kinesis]. Local movements, of course, arrive first at a point midway before reaching their goal (and Sound, it is currently believed, is a movement of something locally moved), but we cannot go on to assert this [arrival at a point midway] like manner of things which undergo qualitative change. For this kind of change may conceivably take place in a thing all at once, without one half of it being changed before the other; e.g. it is conceivable that water should be frozen simultaneously in every part. But still, for all that, if the body which is heated or frozen is extensive, each part of it successively is affected by the part contiguous, while the part first changed in quality is so changed by the cause itself which originates the change, and thus the change throughout the whole need not take place coinstantaneously and all at once. Tasting would have been as smelling now is, if we lived in a liquid medium, and perceived [the sapid object] at a distance, before touching it.

Naturally, then, the parts of media between a sensory organ and its object are not all affected at once– except in the case of Light [illumination] for the reason above stated, and also in the case of seeing, for the same reason; for Light is an efficient cause of seeing.

7

Another question respecting sense–perception is as follows: assuming, as is natural, that of two [simultaneous] sensory stimuli the stronger always tends to extrude the weaker [from consciousness], is it conceivable or not that one should be able to discern two objects coinstantaneously in the same individual time? The above assumption explains why persons do not perceive what is brought before their eyes, if they are at the time deep in thought, or in a fright, or listening to some loud noise. This assumption, then, must be made, and also the following: that it is easier to discern each object of sense when in its simple form than when an ingredient in a mixture; easier, for example, to discern wine when neat than when blended, and so also honey, and [in other provinces] a colour, or to discern the nete by itself alone, than [when sounded with the hypate] in the octave; the reason being that component elements tend to efface [the distinctive characteristics of] one another. Such is the effect [on one another] of all ingredients of which, when compounded, some one thing is formed.

If, then, the greater stimulus tends to expel the less, it necessarily follows that, when they concur, this greater should itself too be less distinctly perceptible than if it were alone, since the less by blending with it has removed some of its individuality, according to our assumption that simple objects are in all cases more distinctly perceptible.

Now, if the two stimuli are equal but heterogeneous, no perception of either will ensue; they will alike efface one another's characteristics. But in such a case the perception of either stimulus in its simple form is impossible. Hence either there will then be no sense–perception at all, or there will be a perception compounded of both and differing from either. The latter is what actually seems to result from ingredients blended together, whatever may be the compound in which they are so mixed.

Since, then, from some concurrent [sensory stimuli] a resultant object is produced, while from others no such resultant is produced, and of the latter sort are those things which belong to different sense provinces (for only those things are capable of mixture whose extremes are contraries, and no one compound can be formed from, e.g. White and Sharp, except indirectly, i.e. not as a concord is formed of Sharp and Grave); there follows logically the impossibility of discerning such concurrent stimuli coinstantaneously. For we must suppose that the stimuli, when equal, tend alike to efface one another, since no one [form of stimulus] results from them; while, if they are unequal, the stronger alone is distinctly perceptible.

Again, the soul would be more likely to perceive coinstantaneously, with one and the same sensory act, two things in the same sensory province, such as the Grave and the Sharp in sound; for the sensory stimulation in this one province is more likely to be unitemporal than that involving two different provinces, as Sight and Hearing. But it is impossible to perceive two objects coinstantaneously in the same sensory act unless they have been mixed, [when, however, they are no longer two], for their amalgamation involves their becoming one, and the sensory act related to one object is itself one, and such act, when one, is, of course, coinstantaneous with itself. Hence, when things are mixed we of necessity perceive them coinstantaneously: for we perceive them by a perception actually one. For an object numerically one means that which is perceived by a perception actually one, whereas an object specifically one means that which is perceived by a sensory act potentially one [i.e. by an energeia of the same sensuous faculty]. If then the actualized perception is one, it will declare its data to be one object; they must, therefore, have been mixed. Accordingly, when they have not been mixed, the actualized perceptions which perceive them will be two; but [if so, their perception must be successive not coinstantaneous, for] in one and the same faculty the perception actualized at any single moment is necessarily one, only one stimulation or exertion of a single faculty being possible at a single instant, and in the case supposed here the faculty is one. It follows, therefore, that we cannot conceive the possibility of perceiving two distinct objects coinstantaneously with one and the same sense.

But if it be thus impossible to perceive coinstantaneously two objects in the same province of sense if they are really two, manifestly it is still less conceivable that we should perceive coinstantaneously objects in two different sensory provinces, as White and Sweet. For it appears that when the Soul predicates numerical unity it does so in virtue of nothing else than such coinstantaneous perception [of one object, in one instant, by one energeia]: while it predicates specific unity in virtue of [the unity of] the discriminating faculty of sense together with [the unity of] the mode in which this operates. What I mean, for example, is this; the same sense no doubt discerns White and Black, [which are hence generically one] though specifically different from one another, and so, too, a faculty of sense self–identical, but different from the former, discerns Sweet and Bitter; but while both these faculties differ from one another [and each from itself] in their modes of discerning either of their respective contraries, yet in perceiving the co–ordinates in each province they proceed in manners analogous to one another; for instance, as Taste perceives Sweet, so Sight perceives White; and as the latter perceives Black, so the former perceives Bitter.

Again, if the stimuli of sense derived from Contraries are themselves Contrary, and if Contraries cannot be conceived as subsisting together in the same individual subject, and if Contraries, e.g. Sweet and Bitter, come under one and the same sense–faculty, we must conclude that it is impossible to discern them coinstantaneously. It is likewise clearly impossible so to discern such homogeneous sensibles as are not [indeed] Contrary, [but are yet of different species]. For these are, [in the sphere of colour, for instance], classed some with White, others with Black, and so it is, likewise, in the other provinces of sense; for example, of savours, some are classed with Sweet, and others with Bitter. Nor can one discern the components in compounds coinstantaneously (for these are ratios of Contraries, as e.g. the Octave or the Fifth); unless, indeed, on condition of perceiving them as one. For thus, and not otherwise, the ratios of the extreme sounds are compounded into one ratio: since we should have together the ratio, on the one hand, of Many to Few or of Odd to Even, on the other, that of Few to Many or of Even to Odd [and these, to be perceived together, must be unified].

If, then, the sensibles denominated co-ordinates though in different provinces of sense (e.g. I call Sweet and White co-ordinates though in different provinces) stand yet more aloof, and differ more, from one another than do any sensibles in the same province; while Sweet differs from White even more than Black does from White, it is still less conceivable that one should discern them [viz. sensibles in different sensory provinces whether co-ordinates or not] coinstantaneously than sensibles which are in the same province. Therefore, if coinstantaneous perception of the latter be impossible, that of the former is a fortiori impossible.

Some of the writers who treat of concords assert that the sounds combined in these do not reach us simultaneously, but only appear to do so, their real successiveness being unnoticed whenever the time it involves is [so small as to be] imperceptible. Is this true or not? One might perhaps, following this up, go so far as to say that even the current opinion that one sees and hears coinstantaneously is due merely to the fact that the intervals of time [between the really successive perceptions of sight and hearing] escape observation. But this can scarcely be true, nor is it conceivable that any portion of time should be [absolutely] imperceptible, or that any should be absolutely unnoticeable; the truth being that it is possible to perceive every instant of time. [This is so]; because, if it is inconceivable that a person should, while perceiving himself or aught else in a continuous time, be at any instant unaware of his own existence; while, obviously, the assumption, that there is in the time-continuum a time so small as to be absolutely imperceptible, carries the implication that a person would, during such time, be unaware of his own existence, as well as of his seeing and perceiving; [this assumption must be false].

Again, if there is any magnitude, whether time or thing, absolutely imperceptible owing to its smallness, it follows that there would not be either a thing which one perceives, or a time in which one perceives it, unless in the sense that in some part of the given time he sees some part of the given thing. For [let there be a line ab, divided into two parts at g, and let this line represent a whole object and a corresponding whole time. Now,] if one sees the whole line, and perceives it during a time which forms one and the same continuum, only in the sense that he does so in some portion of this time, let us suppose the part gb, representing a time in which by supposition he was perceiving nothing, cut off from the whole. Well, then, he perceives in a certain part [viz. in the remainder] of the time, or perceives a part [viz. the remainder] of the line, after the fashion in which one sees the whole earth by seeing some given part of it, or walks in a year by walking in some given part of the year. But [by hypothesis] in the part bg he perceives nothing: therefore, in fact, he is said to perceive the whole object and during the whole time simply because he perceives [some part of the object] in some part of the time ab. But the same argument holds also in the case of ag [the remainder, regarded in its turn as a whole]; for it will be found [on this theory of vacant times and imperceptible magnitudes] that one always perceives only in some part of a given whole time, and perceives only some part of a whole magnitude, and that it is impossible to perceive any [really] whole [object in a really whole time; a conclusion which is absurd, as it would logically annihilate the perception of both Objects and Time].

Therefore we must conclude that all magnitudes are perceptible, but their actual dimensions do not present themselves immediately in their presentation as objects. One sees the sun, or a four–cubit rod at a distance, as a magnitude, but their exact dimensions are not given in their visual presentation: nay, at times an object of sight appears indivisible, but [vision like other special senses, is fallible respecting 'common sensibles', e.g. magnitude, and] nothing that one sees is really indivisible. The reason of this has been previously explained. It is clear then, from the above arguments, that no portion of time is imperceptible.

But we must here return to the question proposed above for discussion, whether it is possible or impossible to perceive several objects coinstantaneously; by 'coinstantaneously' I mean perceiving the several objects in a time one and indivisible relatively to one another, i.e. indivisible in a sense consistent with its being all a continuum.

ON SENSE AND THE SENSIBLE

First, then, is it conceivable that one should perceive the different things coinstantaneously, but each with a different part of the Soul? Or [must we object] that, in the first place, to begin with the objects of one and the same sense, e.g. Sight, if we assume it [the Soul qua exercising Sight] to perceive one colour with one part, and another colour with a different part, it will have a plurality of parts the same in species, [as they must be,] since the objects which it thus perceives fall within the same genus?

Should any one [to illustrate how the Soul might have in it two different parts specifically identical, each directed to a set of aistheta the same in genus with that to which the other is directed] urge that, as there are two eyes, so there may be in the Soul something analogous, [the reply is] that of the eyes, doubtless, some one organ is formed, and hence their actualization in perception is one; but if this is so in the Soul, then, in so far as what is formed of both [i.e. of any two specifically identical parts as assumed] is one, the true perceiving subject also will be one, [and the contradictory of the above hypothesis (of different parts of Soul remaining engaged in simultaneous perception with one sense) is what emerges from the analogy]; while if the two parts of Soul remain separate, the analogy of the eyes will fail, [for of these some one is really formed].

Furthermore, [on the supposition of the need of different parts of Soul, co–operating in each sense, to discern different objects coinstantaneously], the senses will be each at the same time one and many, as if we should say that they were each a set of diverse sciences; for neither will an 'activity' exist without its proper faculty, nor without activity will there be sensation.

But if the Soul does not, in the way suggested [i.e. with different parts of itself acting simultaneously], perceive in one and the same individual time sensibles of the same sense, a fortiori it is not thus that it perceives sensibles of different senses. For it is, as already stated, more conceivable that it should perceive a plurality of the former together in this way than a plurality of heterogeneous objects.

If then, as is the fact, the Soul with one part perceives Sweet, with another, White, either that which results from these is some one part, or else there is no such one resultant. But there must be such an one, inasmuch as the general faculty of sense–perception is one. What one object, then, does that one faculty [when perceiving an object, e.g. as both White and Sweet] perceive? [None]; for assuredly no one object arises by composition of these [heterogeneous objects, such as White and Sweet]. We must conclude, therefore, that there is, as has been stated before, some one faculty in the soul with which the latter perceives all its percepts, though it perceives each different genus of sensibles through a different organ.

May we not, then, conceive this faculty which perceives White and Sweet to be one qua indivisible [sc. qua combining its different simultaneous objects] in its actualization, but different, when it has become divisible [sc. qua distinguishing its different simultaneous objects] in its actualization?

Or is what occurs in the case of the perceiving Soul conceivably analogous to what holds true in that of the things themselves? For the same numerically one thing is white and sweet, and has many other qualities, [while its numerical oneness is not thereby prejudiced] if the fact is not that the qualities are really separable in the object from one another, but that the being of each quality is different [from that of every other]. In the same way therefore we must assume also, in the case of the Soul, that the faculty of perception in general is in itself numerically one and the same, but different [differentiated] in its being; different, that is to say, in genus as regards some of its objects, in species as regards others. Hence too, we may conclude that one can perceive [numerically different objects] coinstantaneously with a faculty which is numerically one and the same, but not the same in its relationship [sc. according as the objects to which it is directed are not the same].

That every sensible object is a magnitude, and that nothing which it is possible to perceive is indivisible, may be thus shown. The distance whence an object could not be seen is indeterminate, but that whence it is visible is determinate. We may say the same of the objects of Smelling and Hearing, and of all sensibles not discerned by actual contact. Now, there is, in the interval of distance, some extreme place, the last from which the object is invisible, and the first from which it is visible. This place, beyond which if the object be one cannot perceive it, while if the object be on the hither side one must perceive it, is, I presume, itself necessarily indivisible. Therefore, if any sensible object be indivisible, such object, if set in the said extreme place whence imperceptibility ends and perceptibility begins, will have to be both visible and invisible their objects, whether regarded in general or at the same time; but this is impossible.

This concludes our survey of the characteristics of the organs of Sense–perception and their objects, whether regarded in general or in relation to each organ. Of the remaining subjects, we must first consider that of memory and remembering.

–THE END–

Printed in the United States
82948LV00004B/3-10/A

9 781419 138577